Measurement Age 5-6

Melissa Blackwood, Liz Dawson & Stephen Monaghan

In a strange place, not too far from here, lives a scare of monsters.

A 'scare' is what some people call a group of monsters, but these monsters are really very friendly once you get to know them.

They are a curious bunch – they look very unusual, but they are quite like you and me, and they love learning new things and having fun.

In this book you will go on a learning journey with the monsters and you are sure to have lots of fun along the way.

Visit our website to meet the monsters and upload your drawings to the Monster Gallery.

Contents

What is a Metre?

Otto and Webber are looking at how to **measure** the length of objects. Otto knows that he can use cubes to measure the length of a line.

This line is 6 cubes long.

Otto now wants to know how long his bed is in cubes.

Otto's bed is 10 cubes long.

Webber tells Otto that we measure large items in **metres**. The abbreviation for metres is **m**.

Webber says that a metre is about the length of your arms when they are stretched out, like the wings of an aeroplane.

1 Help Otto measure these items in cubes.

a

The table is 5 cubes long.

b

The book is 5 cubes long.

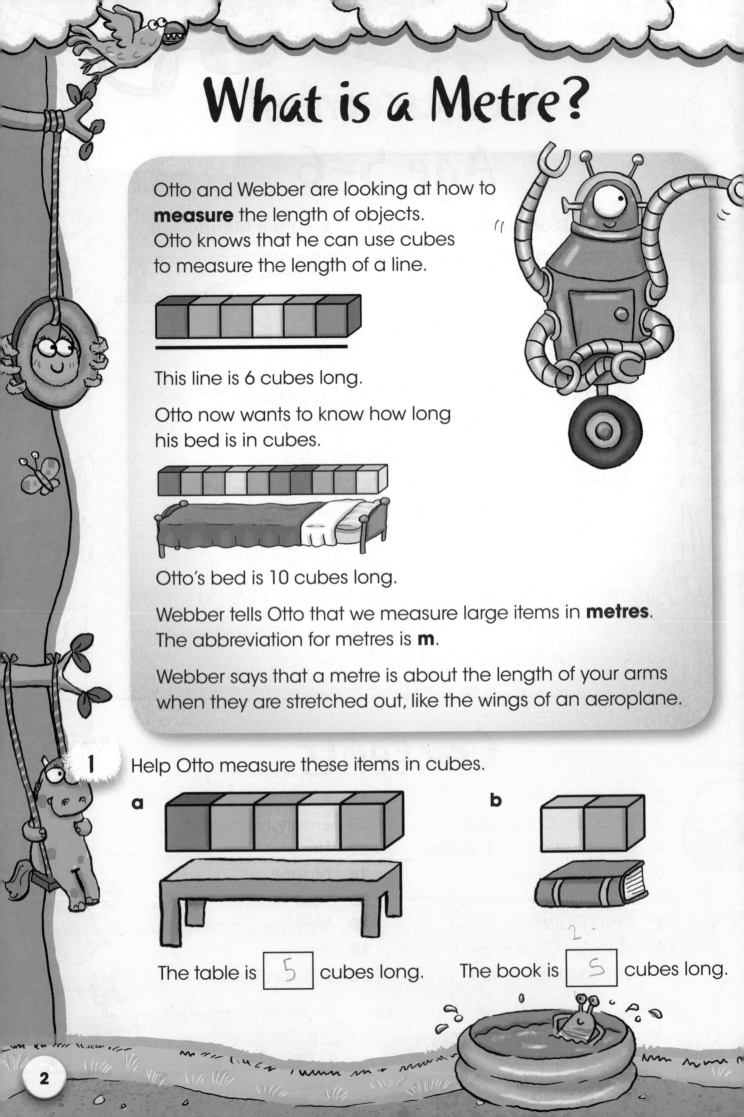

2 Using your 'metre' stretched arms, measure these things.

a The length of your bedroom wall.

The length of my bedroom wall is ☐ m.

b The length of your bookshelf.

The length of my bookshelf is ☐ m.

3 The monsters have had a throwing competition.
Write how far each ball has travelled.

Otto				●		
Tizz		●				
Poggo			●			
Kora	●					
	1 m	2 m	3 m	4 m	5 m	

Otto's ball travelled ☐ m.   Poggo's ball travelled ☐ m.

Tizz's ball travelled ☐ m.   Kora's ball travelled ☐ m.

Fun Zone!

Dance with monster feet.

Super!
You can now find and colour **Shape 1** on the Monster Match page!

Monster Feet

You will need cardboard, paint, string and scissors. Ask an adult to help when needed.

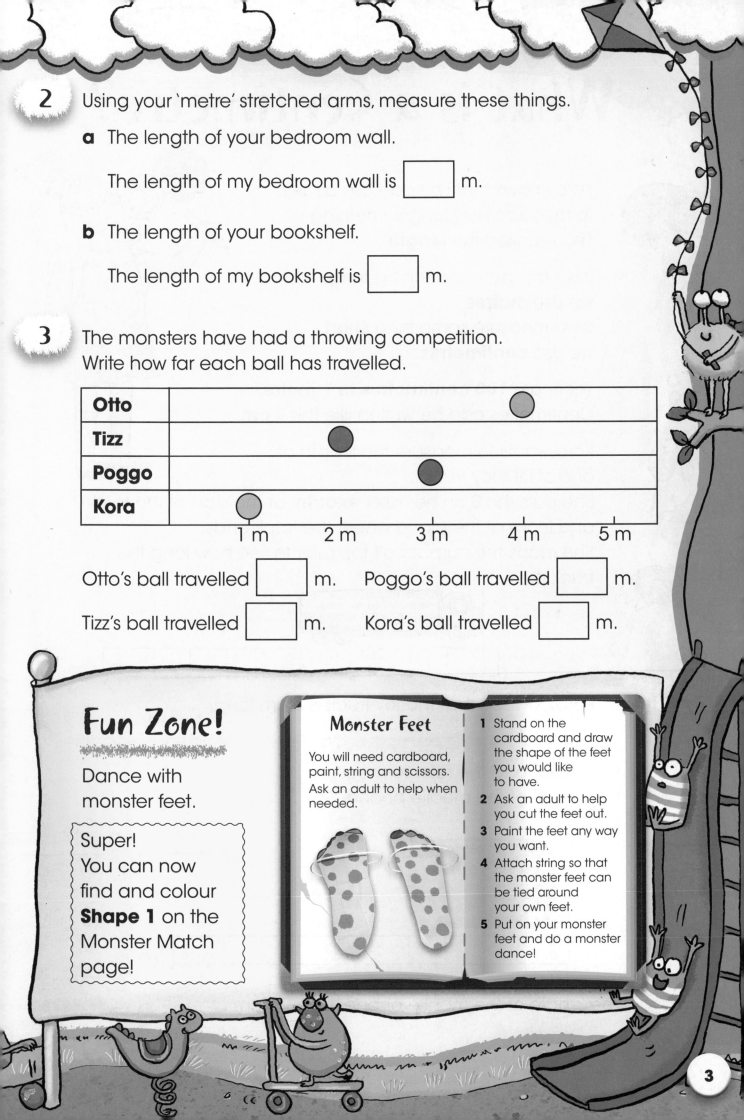

1 Stand on the cardboard and draw the shape of the feet you would like to have.

2 Ask an adult to help you cut the feet out.

3 Paint the feet any way you want.

4 Attach string so that the monster feet can be tied around your own feet.

5 Put on your monster feet and do a monster dance!

What is a Centimetre?

Kora knows that she can use a ruler to measure how long something is. This is called the **length**.

If we measure something **long**, we use **metres**.
If we measure something **short**, we use **centimetres**.

There are **100 centimetres in 1 metre**.
Centimetres can be written like this – **cm**.

Kora wants to measure the length of one of Rif's toy trucks.
She puts the 0 on her ruler **exactly** at the start of the truck and looks at the place where the truck ends.
She reads the number off the ruler to see how long the truck is.

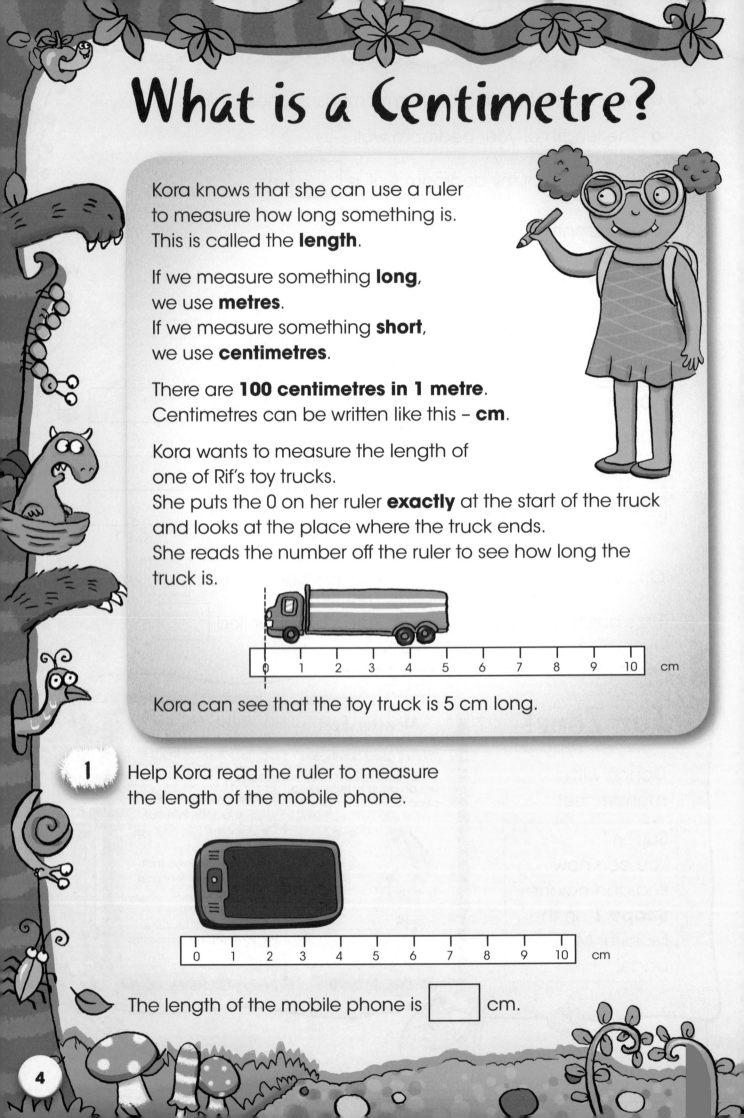

Kora can see that the toy truck is 5 cm long.

1 Help Kora read the ruler to measure the length of the mobile phone.

The length of the mobile phone is ☐ cm.

2 Find objects around your house and measure them carefully. Trace over the ruler below and use it to measure the objects.

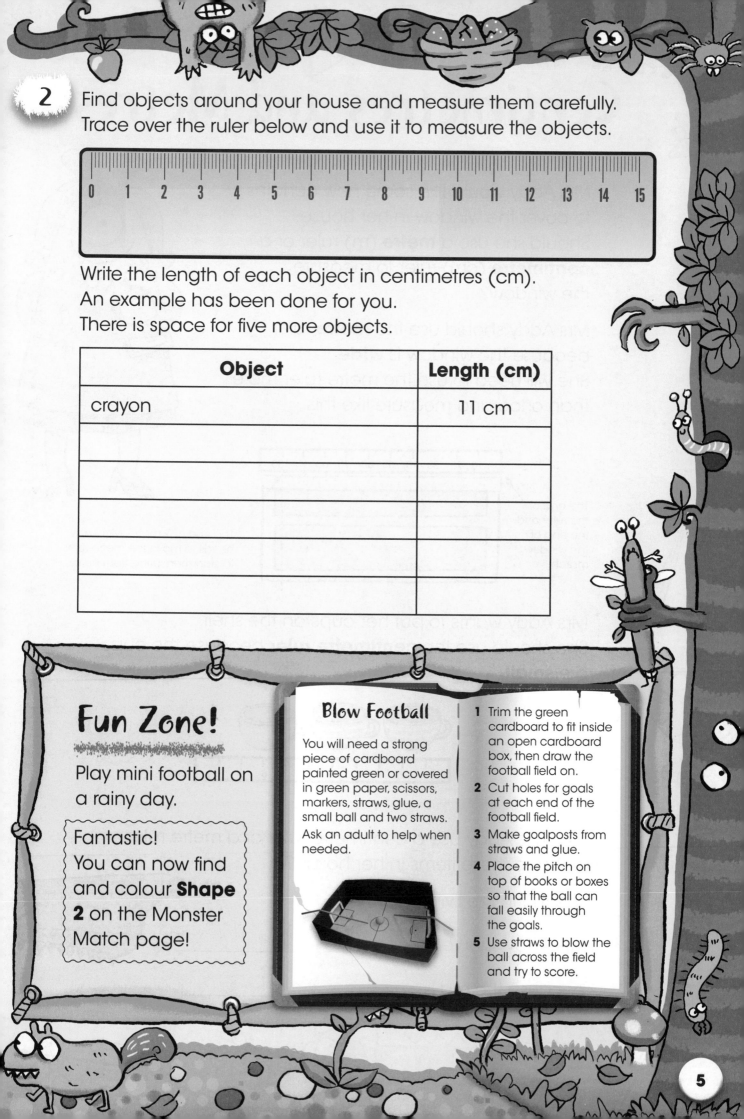

Write the length of each object in centimetres (cm).
An example has been done for you.
There is space for five more objects.

Object	Length (cm)
crayon	11 cm

Fun Zone!

Play mini football on a rainy day.

Fantastic!
You can now find and colour **Shape 2** on the Monster Match page!

Blow Football

You will need a strong piece of cardboard painted green or covered in green paper, scissors, markers, straws, glue, a small ball and two straws.

Ask an adult to help when needed.

1 Trim the green cardboard to fit inside an open cardboard box, then draw the football field on.
2 Cut holes for goals at each end of the football field.
3 Make goalposts from straws and glue.
4 Place the pitch on top of books or boxes so that the ball can fall easily through the goals.
5 Use straws to blow the ball across the field and try to score.

Centimetres and Metres

Mrs Addy would like some new curtains to cover the window in her house. Should she use a **metre** (m) ruler or a **centimetre** (cm) ruler to measure the window?

Mrs Addy should use the **metre** ruler because the window is **wide**.
She will need to use the metre ruler more than once and measure like this.

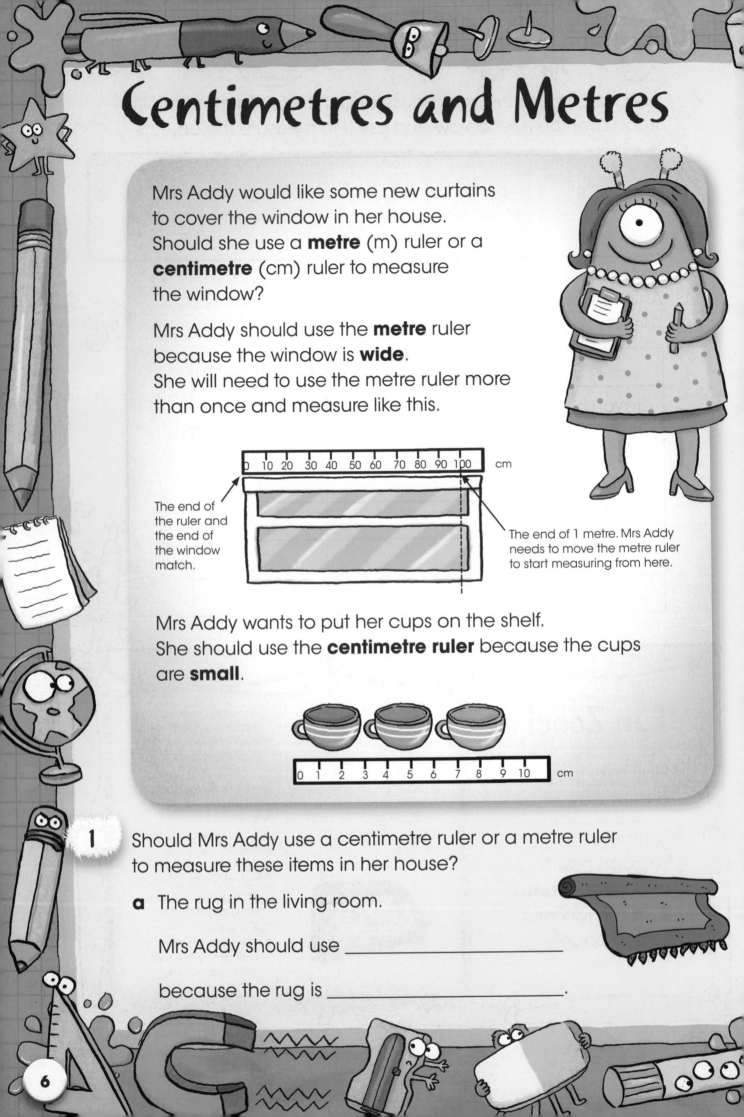

0 10 20 30 40 50 60 70 80 90 100   cm

The end of the ruler and the end of the window match.

The end of 1 metre. Mrs Addy needs to move the metre ruler to start measuring from here.

Mrs Addy wants to put her cups on the shelf.
She should use the **centimetre ruler** because the cups are **small**.

0 1 2 3 4 5 6 7 8 9 10   cm

---

1 Should Mrs Addy use a centimetre ruler or a metre ruler to measure these items in her house?

a The rug in the living room.

Mrs Addy should use _____

because the rug is _____ .

b Mrs Addy's photo album.

Mrs Addy should use _____

because the photo album is _____.

c Mrs Addy's shed.

Mrs Addy should use _____

because the shed is _____.

d Mrs Addy's pencil.

Mrs Addy should use _____

because the pencil is _____.

Fun Zone!

Say the rhyme as you skip.
Say one letter for each jump.
If you trip, find an object starting with that letter, for example, book for b.

Monsterific! You can now find and colour **Shape 3** on the Monster Match page!

ABCs and vegetable goop.
What will I find in the alphabet soup?
A, B, C, D, E, F, G,
H, I, J, K, L, M, N, O, P,
Q, R, S, T, U, V,
W, X, Y and Z.

Height & Length

Otto tells Kora, Litmus and Poggo that they can **compare** the height and length of their mini-monsters. He shows them some examples to help them.

Otto shows them a picture of three houses and compares them.

tall   taller   tallest

Then Otto shows them three plants and compares them.

small   smaller   smallest

Finally Otto compares the length of three cars.

long   longer   longest

1 Help Kora, Litmus and Poggo compare the mini-monsters and creatures they have found.

a Draw lines to join the correct word to each mini-monster.

| small | smaller | smallest |

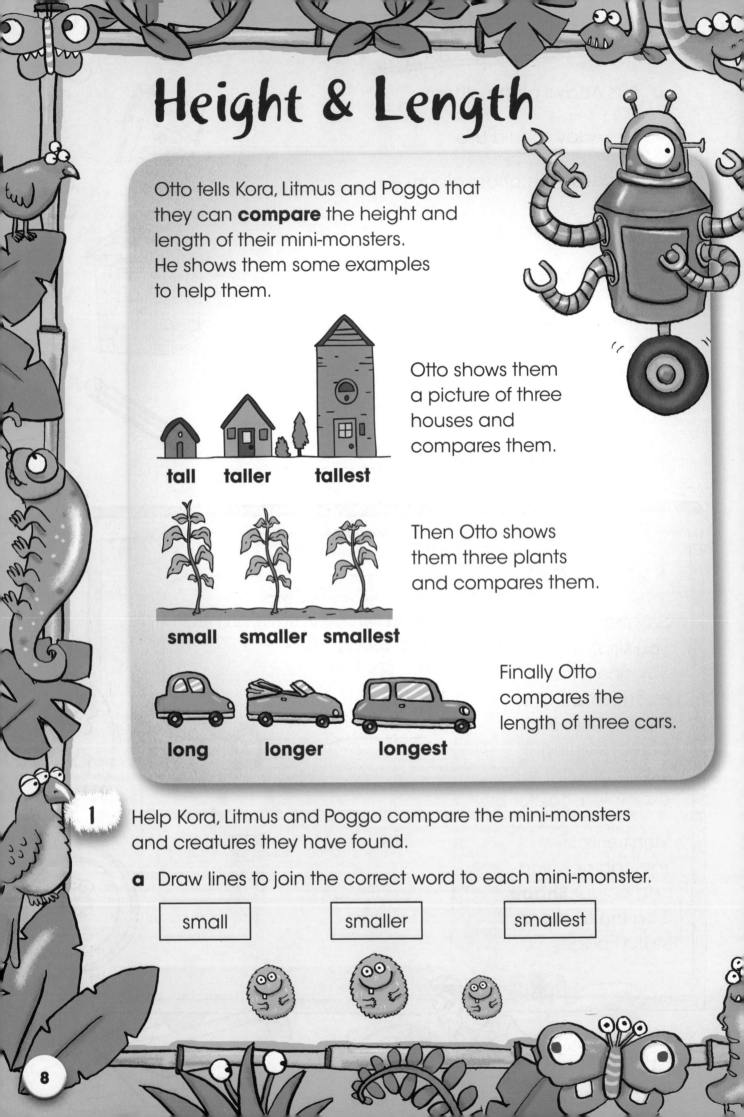

b Draw lines to join the correct word to each mini-monster.

| tall | taller | tallest |

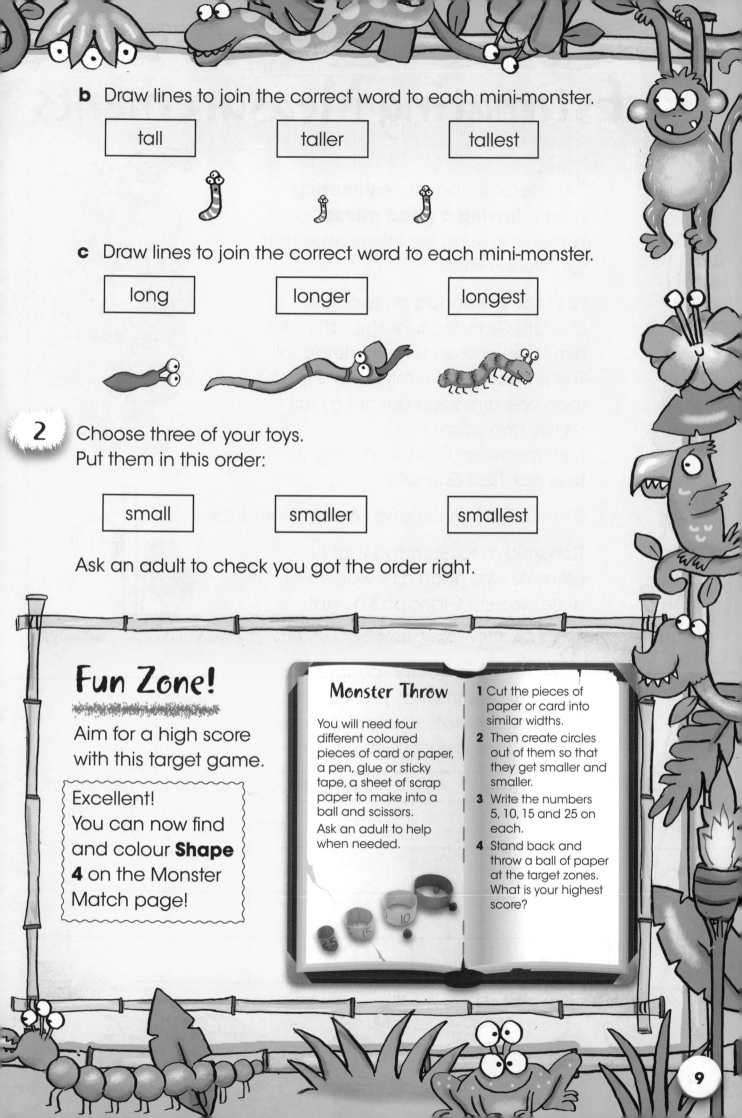

c Draw lines to join the correct word to each mini-monster.

| long | longer | longest |

2 Choose three of your toys.
Put them in this order:

| small | smaller | smallest |

Ask an adult to check you got the order right.

Fun Zone!

Aim for a high score with this target game.

Excellent!
You can now find and colour **Shape 4** on the Monster Match page!

Monster Throw

You will need four different coloured pieces of card or paper, a pen, glue or sticky tape, a sheet of scrap paper to make into a ball and scissors.

Ask an adult to help when needed.

1 Cut the pieces of paper or card into similar widths.

2 Then create circles out of them so that they get smaller and smaller.

3 Write the numbers 5, 10, 15 and 25 on each.

4 Stand back and throw a ball of paper at the target zones. What is your highest score?

Estimating Measurements

Tizz tells Grandpa that **estimating** means **having a good guess** about something using the information that we already know.

Tizz shows Grandpa an example. She tells Grandpa that she estimates him to be one and a half metres tall. This is because she thinks he is taller than one arm span but not as tall as two arm spans.
Kora measures Grandpa's height to check Tizz's estimate.

Grandpa is 1 metre and 76 centimetres tall.

1.76

Tizz explains to Grandpa that her estimate was good as it was quite close to Grandpa's height.

1 Estimate the height of the people in your family.
Fill in the table with what you think their heights are.
Check how accurate your estimation was by measuring their heights with a ruler.

Name	Estimate	Actual measurement

2 Estimate the length of these objects.
Draw a line to match the object to the estimated length.

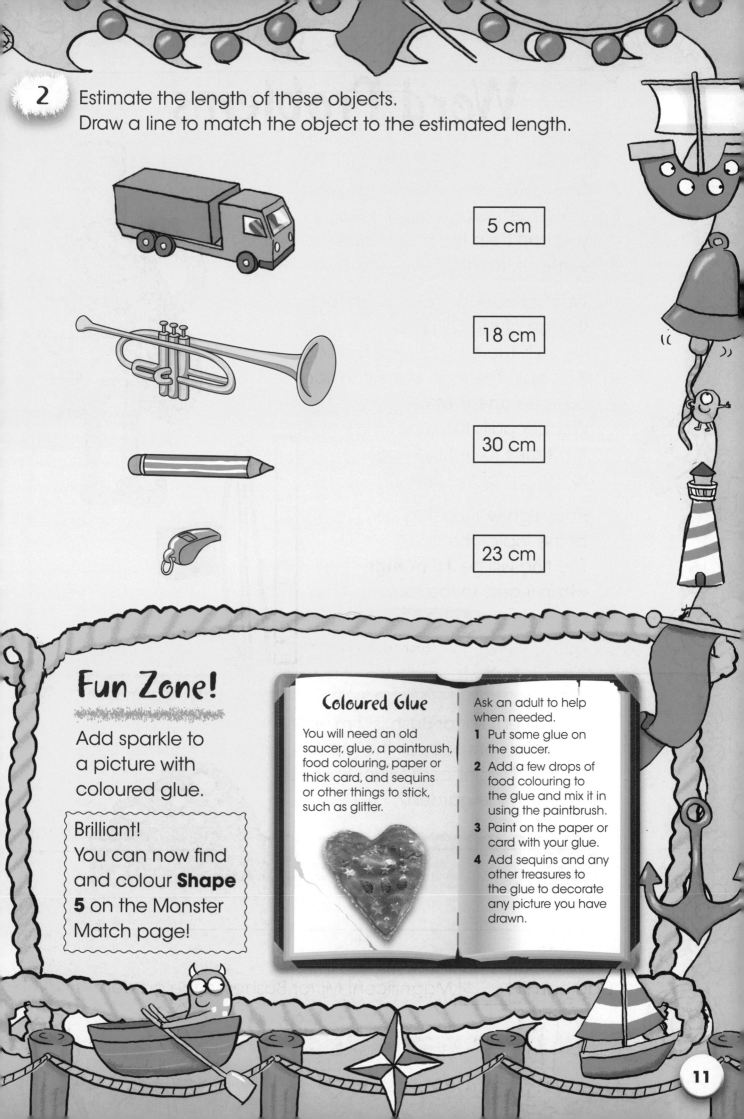

5 cm

18 cm

30 cm

23 cm

Fun Zone!

Add sparkle to a picture with coloured glue.

Brilliant!
You can now find and colour **Shape 5** on the Monster Match page!

Coloured Glue

You will need an old saucer, glue, a paintbrush, food colouring, paper or thick card, and sequins or other things to stick, such as glitter.

Ask an adult to help when needed.

1 Put some glue on the saucer.

2 Add a few drops of food colouring to the glue and mix it in using the paintbrush.

3 Paint on the paper or card with your glue.

4 Add sequins and any other treasures to the glue to decorate any picture you have drawn.

Word Problems

Now you know how to measure using metres and centimetres, you can help the monsters solve some problems.

Webber needs to get a flag to the top of the flag pole.
He pulls the rope to raise the flag.
If he pulls the rope once, the flag goes up **one metre**.
Webber pulls the rope **ten times** to get the flag to the top of the pole.

How high will the flag be at the top of the pole?
The flag will be **10 m high** when it gets to the top.

Each pull is 1 m.

1 A Magnificent Mirror Bush is 2 m wide.
Dad has 6 m of space in the garden.
How many Magnificent Mirror Bushes can he fit in the garden?

2 m

6 m

Dad can fit ☐ Magnificent Mirror Bushes in the garden.

2 Mr Pepper has some photographs to hang in his office.
Each frame is 10 cm wide.

Mr Pepper has 50 cm of space on his wall.
How many photographs can he fit in?

10 cm

50 cm

Mr Pepper can fit [　] photographs on the wall.

3 Webber is measuring the heights of Leckie and Zak.

Zak is 70 cm tall.   Leckie is 50 cm tall.

a Which pet is taller?   [　　　　　　] is taller.

b How much taller?   [　] cm taller.

Fun Zone!

Find all the measurement words in this wordsearch.

Well done!
You can now find and colour **Shape 6** on the Monster Match page!

METRE
SHORT
RULER
TALL
WIDE
LONG

L	R	G	E	T	O	A	R
I	L	D	N	C	T	E	N
H	I	A	I	O	L	T	A
W	M	C	T	U	L	R	C
M	E	T	R	E	W	D	N
S	H	O	R	T	W	I	S
R	M	T	I	A	E	M	T
E	G	T	L	C	O	N	D

Monster Challenge 1

1 Write down if you would measure the following objects in metres (m) or centimetres (cm).

a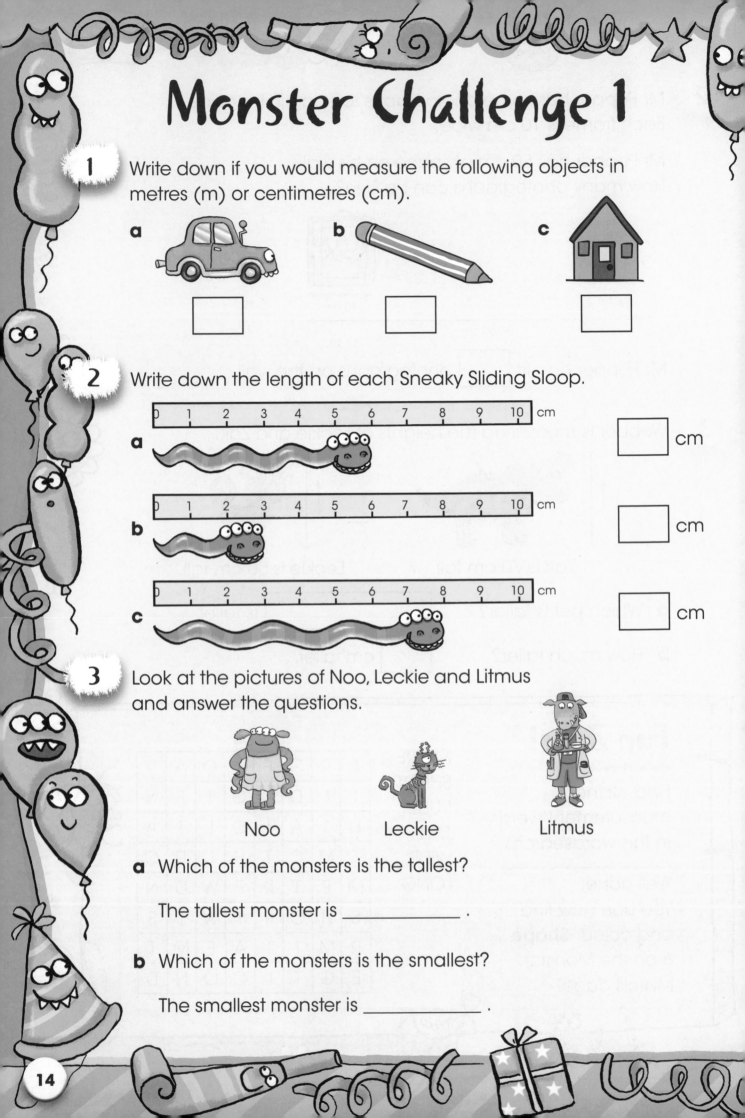

b

c

2 Write down the length of each Sneaky Sliding Sloop.

a

| 0 | 1 | 2 | 3 | 4 | 5 | 6 | 7 | 8 | 9 | 10 | cm |

☐ cm

b

| 0 | 1 | 2 | 3 | 4 | 5 | 6 | 7 | 8 | 9 | 10 | cm |

☐ cm

c

| 0 | 1 | 2 | 3 | 4 | 5 | 6 | 7 | 8 | 9 | 10 | cm |

☐ cm

3 Look at the pictures of Noo, Leckie and Litmus and answer the questions.

Noo   Leckie   Litmus

a Which of the monsters is the tallest?

The tallest monster is _____ .

b Which of the monsters is the smallest?

The smallest monster is _____ .

4 Estimate and then measure the height of the following.

a A door in your house.

Estimate

Actual measurement

b A window in your house.

Estimate

Actual measurement

5 Look at the pictures of Tizz and Fizz, then answer the questions.

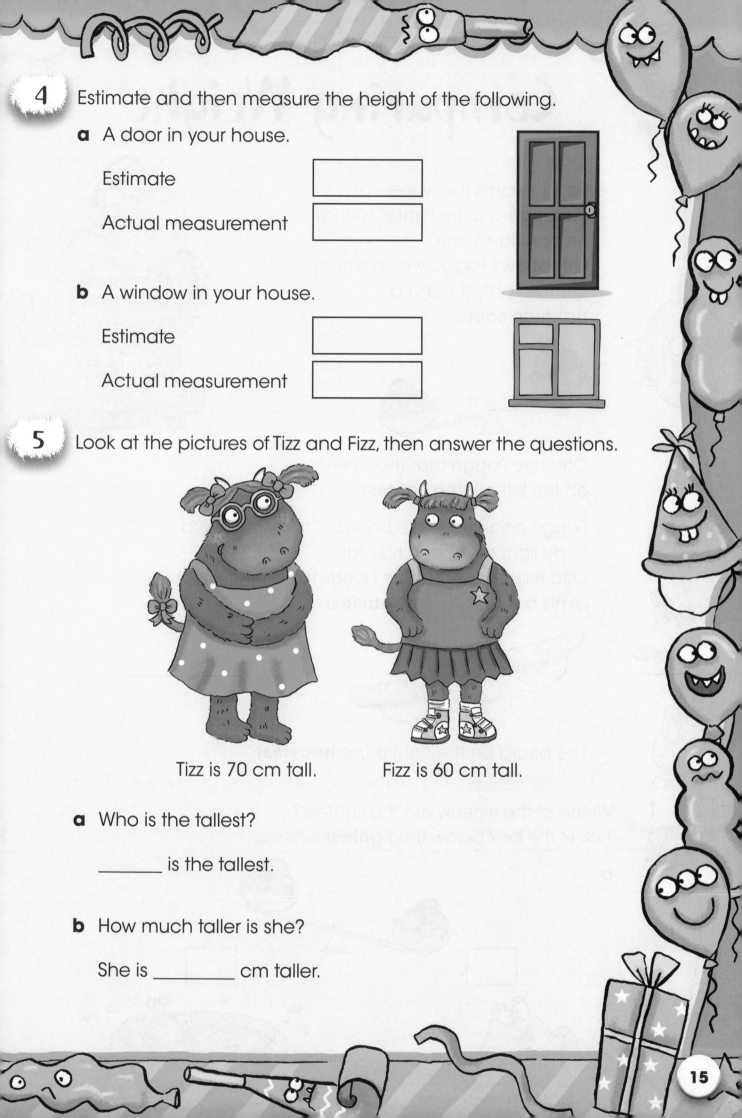

Tizz is 70 cm tall.   Fizz is 60 cm tall.

a Who is the tallest?

_____ is the tallest.

b How much taller is she?

She is _____ cm taller.

Comparing Weight

Poggo wants the wheels of his skateboard to be lighter so that he can ride faster.
Otto shows Poggo which wheels are the lightest using a **balance scale**.

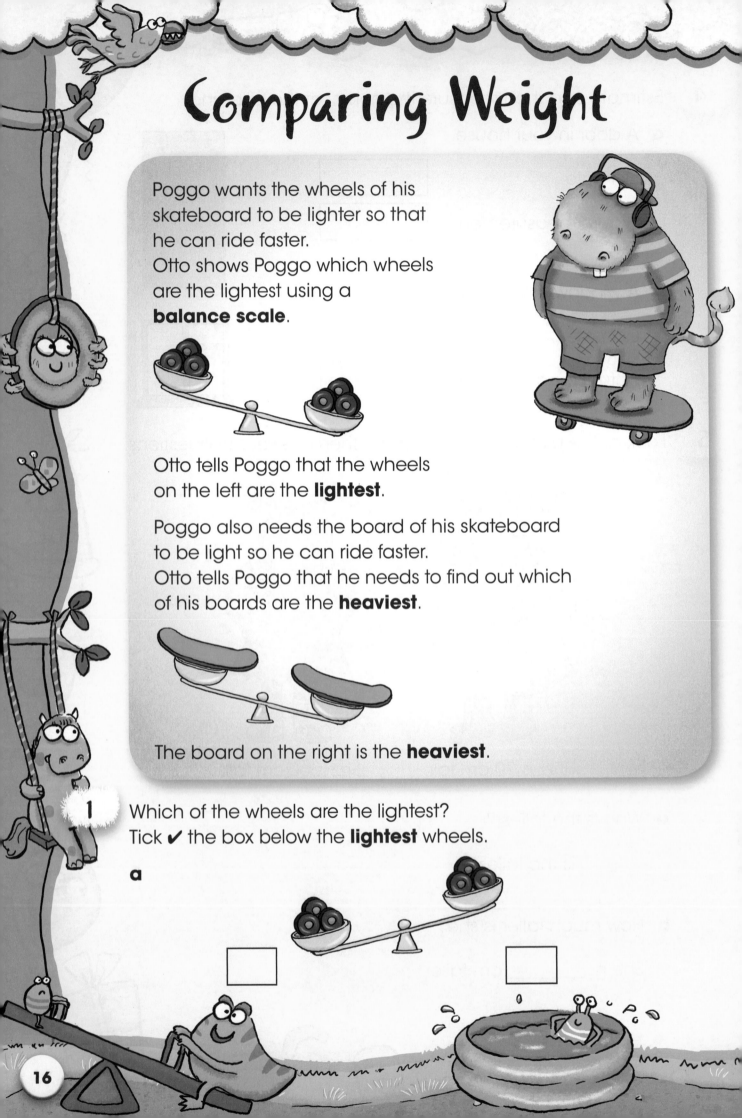

Otto tells Poggo that the wheels on the left are the **lightest**.

Poggo also needs the board of his skateboard to be light so he can ride faster.
Otto tells Poggo that he needs to find out which of his boards are the **heaviest**.

The board on the right is the **heaviest**.

1 Which of the wheels are the lightest?
Tick ✔ the box below the **lightest** wheels.

a

b

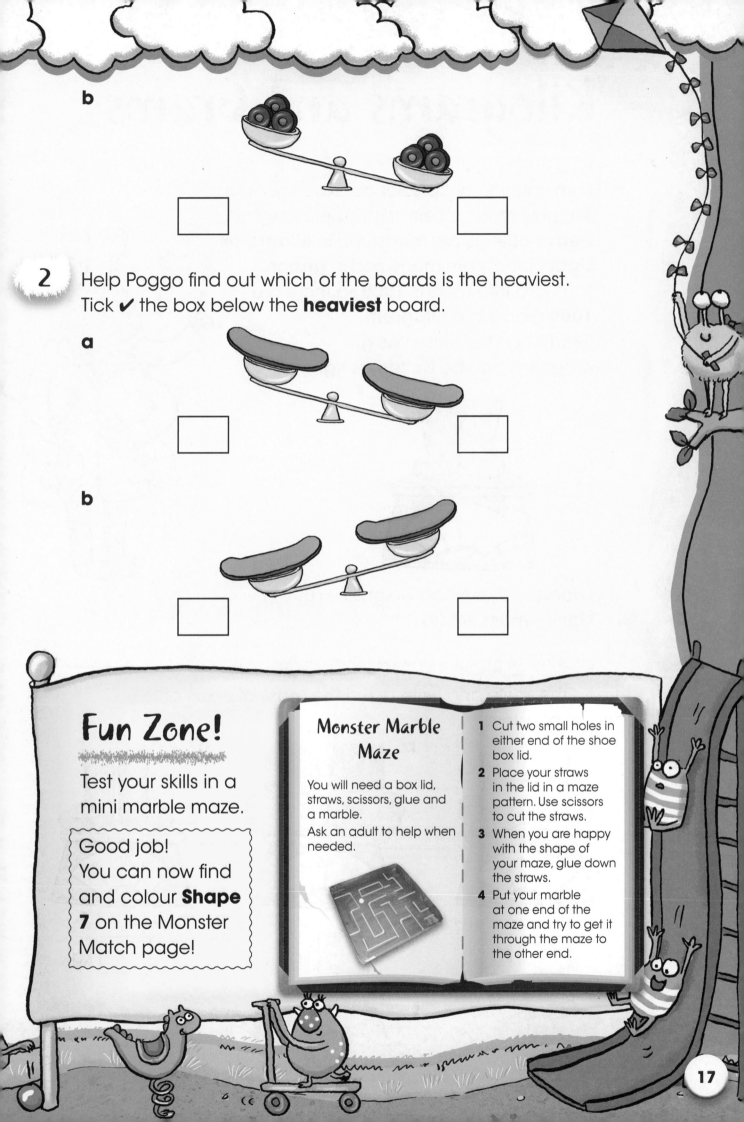

☐　　　☐

2 Help Poggo find out which of the boards is the heaviest.
Tick ✔ the box below the **heaviest** board.

a

☐　　　☐

b

☐　　　☐

Fun Zone!

Test your skills in a mini marble maze.

Good job!
You can now find and colour **Shape 7** on the Monster Match page!

Monster Marble Maze

You will need a box lid, straws, scissors, glue and a marble.
Ask an adult to help when needed.

1 Cut two small holes in either end of the shoe box lid.
2 Place your straws in the lid in a maze pattern. Use scissors to cut the straws.
3 When you are happy with the shape of your maze, glue down the straws.
4 Put your marble at one end of the maze and try to get it through the maze to the other end.

Kilograms and Grams

I am carrying out a science experiment to see how much different monsters weigh. **Heavy** objects are measured in **kilograms**. **Light** objects are measured in **grams**. The word **kilo** means **1000** so there are **1000** grams in a **kilogram**. Grams can be written as **g**. Kilograms can be written as **kg**.

I can see that Nano weighs 6 kg.
Nano's **mass** is 6 kg.

1 Read the scale and write down the mass of each of these monsters.

a

b

c

5 6 7

49 50 51

64 65 66

29 30 31

☐ kg

☐ kg

☐ kg

2 Help the Professor work out the mass of these objects.
Write the mass in the answer box.

a

b

c

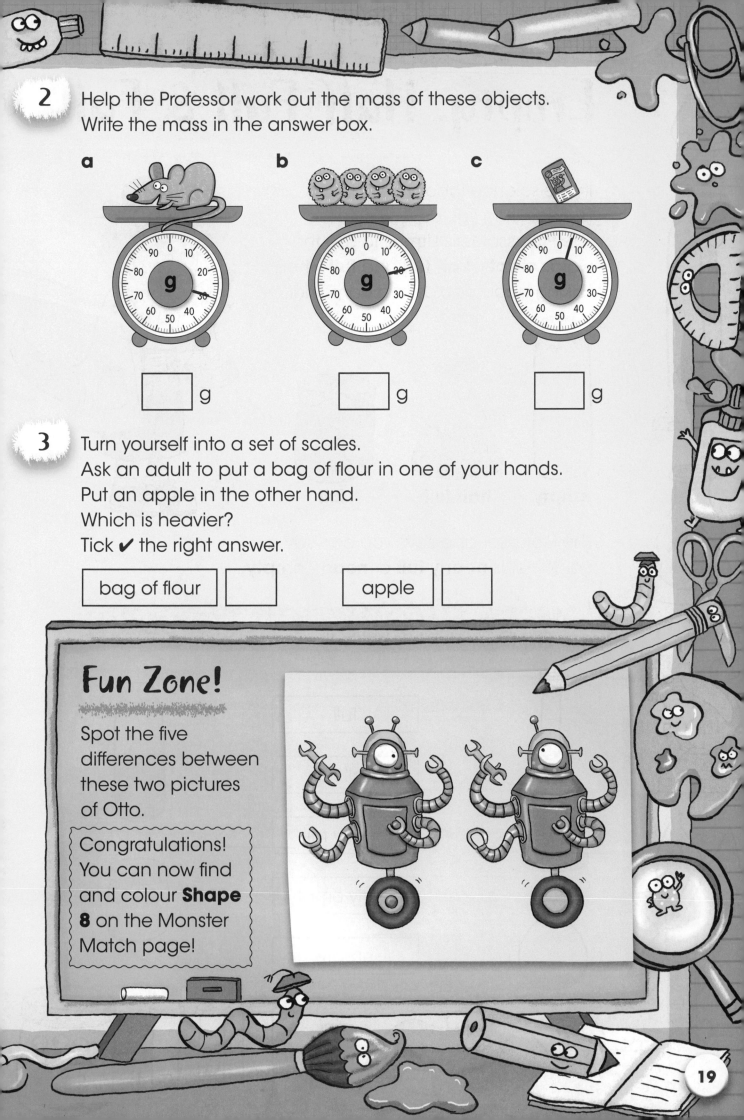

☐ g

☐ g

☐ g

3 Turn yourself into a set of scales.
Ask an adult to put a bag of flour in one of your hands.
Put an apple in the other hand.
Which is heavier?
Tick ✔ the right answer.

bag of flour	☐		apple	☐

Fun Zone!

Spot the five
differences between
these two pictures
of Otto.

Congratulations!
You can now find
and colour **Shape
8** on the Monster
Match page!

Empty, Half Full & Full

In the science laboratory, Litmus is measuring liquids.
The Professor tells Litmus to use the words **empty**, **half full** and **full** when talking about liquids in a container.

empty   half full   full

The Professor also says you can say a container is **nearly full** or **nearly empty**.

1 Draw a line to join each label to the correct picture.

full

half full

nearly full

nearly empty

empty

2 Litmus is trying to make a Beard Growing Potion but he has forgotten what the ingredients are! Read the clues below and write a label for each ingredient.

- Add a half-full tube of snukwater.

- Put in the full container of beetlejuice.

- Add the tub of earwax that is nearly empty.

- Mix it all together and rub on the skin where you would like the beard to grow.

Check the answer page, and if you labelled the ingredients correctly, draw a beard on Litmus!

Fun Zone!

Make your own bouncy ball.

Very good! You can now find and colour **Shape 9** on the Monster Match page!

Elastic Band Ball

You will need newspaper and lots and lots of elastic bands.

Ask an adult to help when needed.

1 Crumple up the newspaper into a little ball. This will be the very middle of the ball.

2 Now start to wind the elastic bands around the newspaper ball and keep going until it is completely covered.

3 Test your bouncy ball.

4 You can keep adding to your bouncy ball as you find more elastic bands.

Litres

The Professor tells Litmus that he is now ready to measure using **litres**.
Litres are the unit of measure used for things you can **pour**.
The short way of writing **litres** is with an **l**.

1 Tick ✔ the items you would measure in litres.

☐ ☐ ☐ ☐

2 What can you find in your house that is measured in litres?
Fill in the table.
Try to find out how much is in the containers.

Container	How many litres?

3 How many litres are in each container?
Write the answers in the boxes.

a

[   ] *l*

b

[   ] *l*

c

[   ] *l*

4 Dad has a bucket that holds 5 litres of water when it is full.
Dad needs 20 litres of water to wash his car.
How many full buckets of water will Dad need?

[   ] buckets

Fun Zone!

Make a bracelet
or necklace out
of paper.

Monsterific!
You can now find
and colour **Shape
10** on the Monster
Match page!

Paper Beads

You will need wrapping
paper or coloured
pages torn from an
old magazine, glue, a
paintbrush with a thin
handle and string.

Ask an adult to help when
needed.

1 Cut long strips of paper.
2 Take a strip of paper
  and glue one side.
3 Place the end of the
  unglued side of the
  strip against the brush
  handle.
4 Carefully wrap the
  paper around the
  handle of the brush,
  one layer of paper
  on top of the other, to
  make a paper bead.
5 Leave the bead to dry.
6 When you have made
  lots of beads, you can
  thread them together
  to make decorations
  or jewellery.

Money

Fizz is beginning to learn all about monster money.
She wants to know who has the most money.
She asks Mum for help.
Mum shows Fizz the money in her purse:

4 × 1 monster pennies

3 × 2 monster pennies

2 × 5 monster pennies

2 × 10 monster pennies

Mum tells Fizz that if she adds up all the money in her purse she has **40** monster pennies.

1 Fizz now wants to know how much money is in the monster purses.
Help Fizz to count the monster money in each purse or wallet.

a Dad's wallet

Dad has [   ] monster pennies.

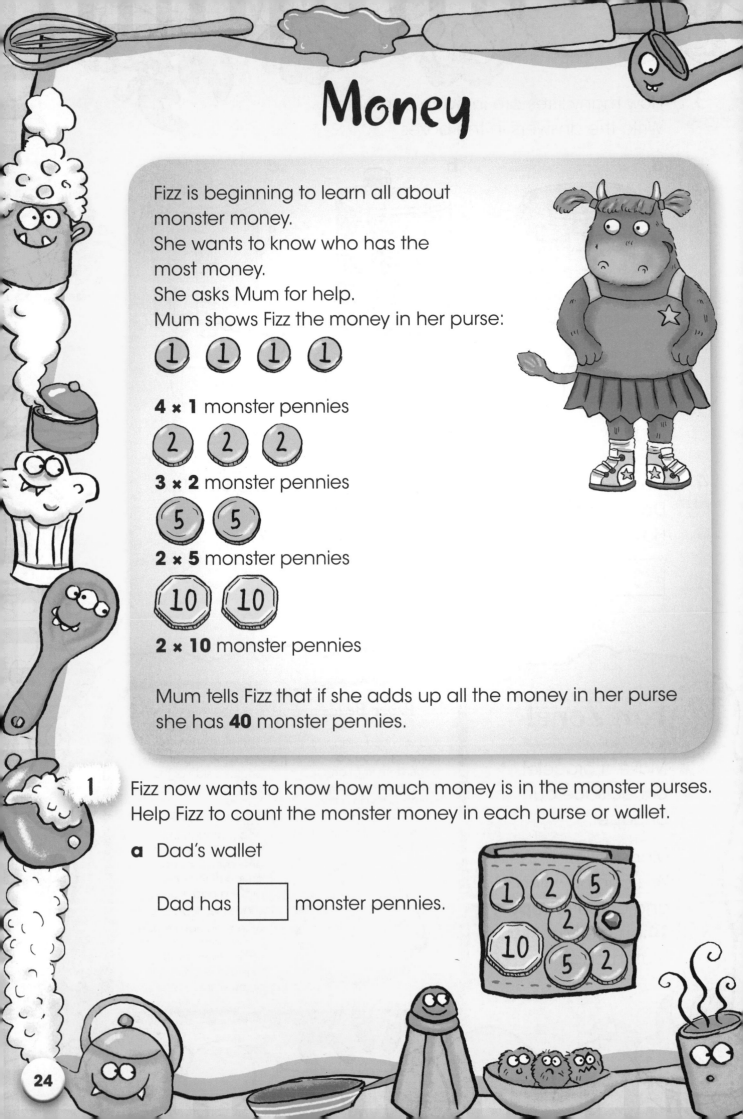

b Gran's purse

Gran has ⬚ monster pennies.

c Litmus' wallet

Litmus has ⬚ monster pennies.

d Kora's purse

Kora has ⬚ monster pennies.

2 Which monster has the most money in their purse or wallet?

_____ has the most money.

Fun Zone!

Join the dots in order to reveal a picture.

Brilliant!
You can now find and colour **Shape 11** on the Monster Match page!

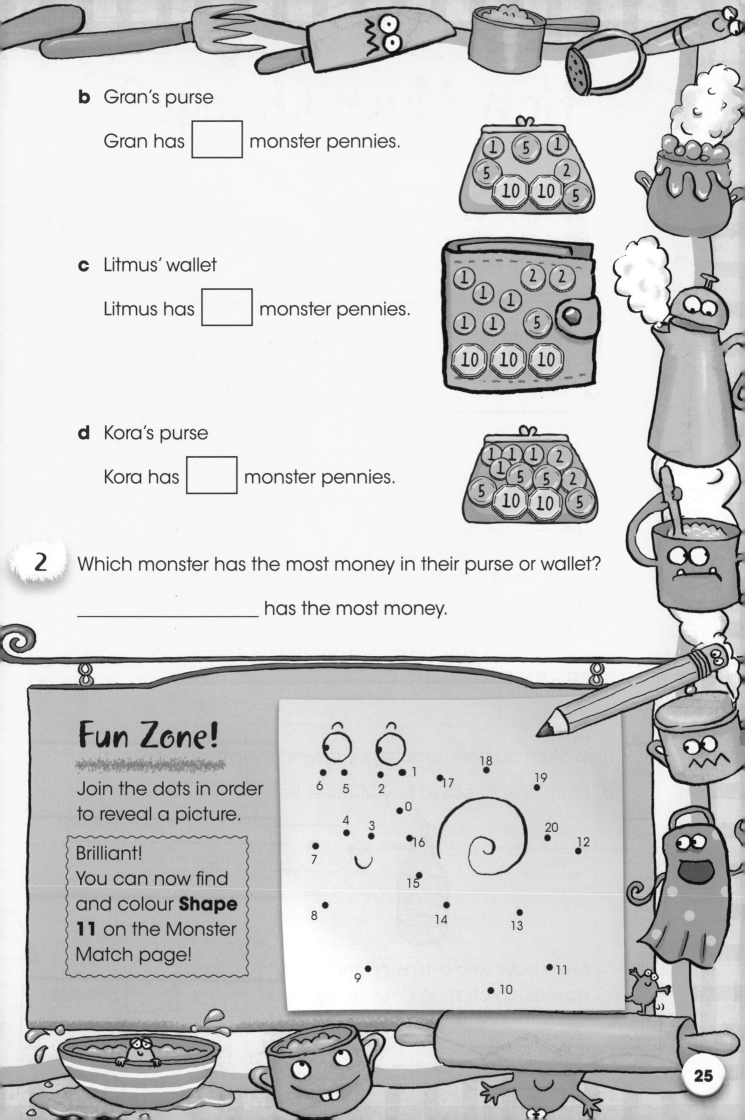

25

How Much Change?

Mum is going shopping.
She has made a shopping
list of all the things she needs
to buy for Kora's birthday.

balloons   mini-monsters
Monster Fizz   a DVD

Mum needs to make sure she takes
her monster pennies.
First, she needs to go and buy some
balloons for Kora's birthday party.
In the shop, Mum finds the balloons she wants.
They cost **4** monster pennies.
Mum has a **10** monster penny.
The shopkeeper gives her **6** monster pennies in change.
Mum knows that this is the right amount of change because
10 − 4 = 6.

1 Help Mum do her shopping by buying everything else on her list.

a Mum now needs to buy Monster Fizz.

8

Mum pays with a 10 monster penny.
How much change does she get?

☐ pennies

b Mum then goes to buy some mini-monsters for Kora's present.

16

She pays with a 20 monster penny.
How much change does she get?

[ ] pennies

2 After that, Mum buys a DVD for Kora.
Now that she has some change,
she can pay with the **exact money**.
Circle the coins that Mum could use to pay for the DVD.

13

20   1   5   10   2

1   5   1   2   10

Fun Zone!

Make a monster of your own.

Good job!
You can now find and colour **Shape 12** on the Monster Match page!

Monster Cup

You will need one plain paper cup, strips of paper (about 2 centimetres wide and 6 centimetres long), paint and glue.

Ask an adult to help when needed.

1 Turn the cup upside down.
2 Stick strips of paper inside the cup for legs.
3 Paint your cup monster.
4 Draw or paint eyes, a mouth and a nose on your monster – or ten eyes, two mouths and no nose!

Monster Challenge 2

1 Which of the mini-monsters is the **heaviest**?

A   B

[ ] is the **heaviest** mini-monster.

2 Which of the mini monsters is the **lightest**?

B   A

[ ] is the **lightest** mini-monster.

3 How much does each mini-monster weigh?

a

[ ] g

b

[ ] g

c

[ ] kg

d

[ ] kg

4 How much potion has Litmus put in each bucket?

a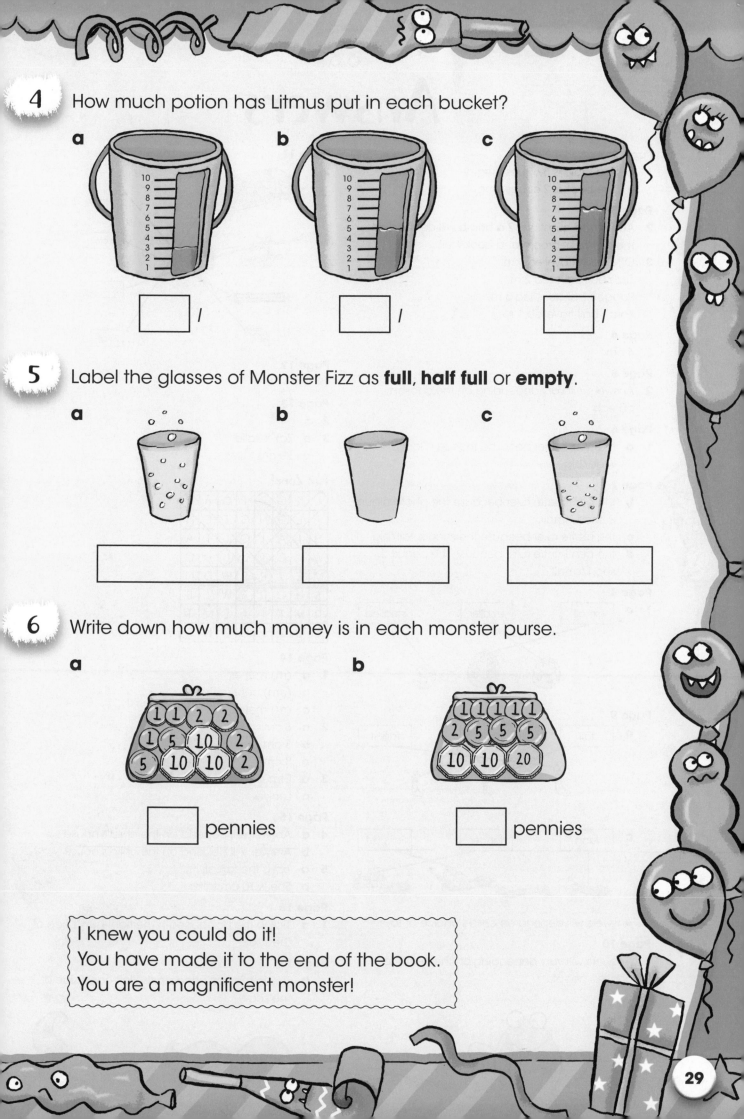

b

c

☐ /   ☐ /   ☐ /

5 Label the glasses of Monster Fizz as **full**, **half full** or **empty**.

a   **b**   **c**

☐   ☐   ☐

6 Write down how much money is in each monster purse.

a   **b**

☐ pennies   ☐ pennies

I knew you could do it!
You have made it to the end of the book.
You are a magnificent monster!

Answers

Page 2

1 a The table is 5 cubes long.

b The book is 2 cubes long.

Page 3

2 Answers to questions 2 **a** and **b** will depend on the child's bedroom and bookshelf

3 Otto's ball travelled 4 m.

Tizz's ball travelled 2 m.

Poggo's ball travelled 3 m.

Kora's ball travelled 1 m.

Page 4

1 4 cm

Page 5

2 Answers will vary depending on the chosen objects

Page 6

1 a the metre ruler because the rug is long/wide/big.

Page 7

b the centimetre ruler because the photo album is short/small.

c the metre ruler because the shed is tall/big.

d the centimetre ruler because the pencil is short/small.

Page 8

1 a

Page 9

b

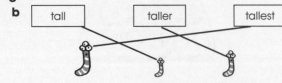

c

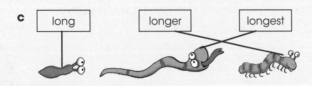

2 Answers will depend on child's choice of toys

Page 10

1 Answers will vary depending on the height of chosen people

Page 11

2

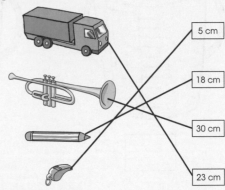

Page 12

1 3

Page 13

2 5

3 a Zak is taller

b 20 cm taller

Fun Zone!

L	R	G	E	T	O	A	R
I	L	D	N	C	T	E	N
H	I	A	I	O	L	T	A
W	M	C	T	U	L	R	C
M	E	T	R	E	W	D	N
S	H	O	R	T	W	I	S
R	M	T	I	A	E	M	T
E	G	T	L	C	O	N	D

Page 14

1 a (m) metres

b (cm) centimetres

c (m) metres

2 a 6 cm

b 3 cm

c 8 cm

3 a Litmus

b Leckie

Page 15

4 a Answer will depend on the child's house

b Answer will depend on the child's house

5 a Tizz is the tallest.

b She is 10 cm taller.

Page 16

1 a Tick in the box beneath the right-hand side of the scale

Page 17

b Tick in the box beneath the left-hand side of the scale

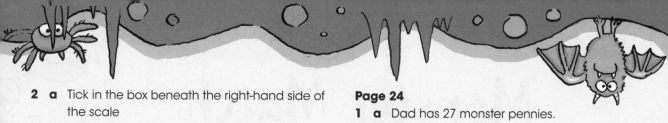

2 a Tick in the box beneath the right-hand side of the scale

b Tick in the box beneath the left-hand side of the scale

Page 18
1 a 50 kg

b 65 kg

c 30 kg

Page 19
2 a 30 g

b 20 g

c 5 g

3 Tick, ✔ the bag of flour

Fun Zone!

Page 20
1

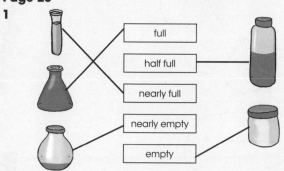

Page 21
2

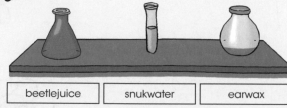

Page 22
1 Bath and paddling pool should be ticked

2 Table dependant on objects chosen

Page 23
3 a 3 litres

b 1 litre

c 7 litres

4 4 buckets

Page 24
1 a Dad has 27 monster pennies.

Page 25
b Gran has 39 monster pennies.

c Litmus has 44 monster pennies.

d Kora has 48 monster pennies.

2 Kora

Fun Zone!

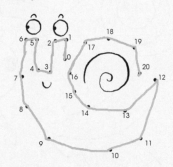

Page 26
1 a 2 pennies

Page 27
b 4 pennies

2

Other combinations are possible

Page 28
1 A

2 B

3 a 30 g

b 60 g

c 3 kg

d 2 kg

Page 29
4 a 3 litres

b 5 litres

c 7 litres

5 a Full

b Empty

c Half full

6 a 51 pennies

b 62 pennies

Monster Match

Each time you complete a topic in this book, you will be awarded a shape number.

Find and colour the shapes in the picture of the monster butterfly that match the numbers you have been given.

As you work through the book you will gradually see the monster butterfly come to life!